The Poetry Of Us

Joshua Rhoades

Published by Joshua Paul Rhoades, 2025.

THE POETRY OF US

First edition. February 7, 2025.

ISBN: 979-8230520115

Written by Joshua Rhoades.

Also by Joshua Rhoades

A Life of Service
When Faith Rolls Up It's Sleeves
Love That Walks The Extra Mile
When Hope Feels Heavy, But Still Holds On

Leadership Series
The Law Of Vision Seeing Beyond The Horizon

The Law of
The The Law of Communication Words That Build Or Break

Standalone
Courage Under Fire: David's Stand On The Battlefield
Jonah's Journey: Voices Of Redemption And Lessons In Obedience
The Furnace Of Faith: 12 Principles From The Heat Of Faith

Whispers of Hope: Inspiring Stories of Men's Prayers In Scripture
Frontier Legends: The Oregon Dream
Elijah: A Beacon Of Boldness
HOOK, LINE & SAVIOUR - Faith Reflections from Fishing
Driven By Faith: Motor Racing Inspired Christian Life
30 Day Devotional - Bold and Strong- Coffee Devotions for a Courageous Christian Walk
Authentic Christianity: The Heart of Old Time Religion
Consider The Ant - God's Tiny Preachers
Flee Fornication: The Plea For Purity
Renewed Hope- How to Find Encouragement in God
Sounding The Call - The Voice of Conviction
The Altar - Where Heaven Meets Earth
The Bible's Battlefields- Timeless Lessons from Ancient Wars
The Sacred Art of Silence - How Silence Speaks in Scripture
Under Fire- The Sanctity of the Traditional Biblical Home
Who Is on the Lord's Side? A Call to Righteousness
What Is Truth? - From Skepticism to Submission
First and Goal- Faith and Football Fundamentals
From Dugout to Devotion- Spiritual Lessons from Baseball
Par for the Course- Faith and Fairways
The Believer's Pace- Tools for Running Life's Marathon
The Immutable Fortress- Security in God's Unchanging Nature
Biblical Bravery
Deer Stands and Devotions: A Hunter's Walk with God
Jesus Knows- Our Hearts, Our Responsibility
Restoration - Setting The Bone
Spiritual 911- God's Word for Life's Emergency's
The Freedom of Forgiveness
The Jezebel Effect - Ancient Manipulations Modern Lessons

The Shout That Stopped The Saviour
The Time Machine Chronicles: Old Testament Characters
Anchored In Truth Exploring The Depths of Psalm 119
Biblical Counsel on Anger
Proverbs' Portraits The Men God Mentions
Stumbling in the Dark - The Dangers of Alcohol
Guarding the Wicket Protecting Your Faith and Game
The Champion's Faith - Wrestling and Achieving Spiritual Victory
Scriptural Commands for Modern Times Living God's Word Today Volume 1
Scriptural Commands for Modern Times Living God's Word Today Volume 2
Scriptural Commands for Modern Times Living God's Word TodayVolume3
The Greatest Gift
A Christmas Journey of Faith
Daughter Of The King: Embracing Your Identity In Christ
Determination and Dedication Building Strong Faith As A Young Man
Walking Through Walls God's Power to Part the Storms of Life
David's Song Of Deliverance Praising God Through Every Storm
From Weakness to Warrior: Gideon's Transformation
Why Did Jesus Weep?
Living For God The Call To Be A Living Sacrifice
My Mind Is In A Fog What Do I Do?
Turning The Page Written By Grace
The Calling and Greatness of John the Baptist
For Such a Time Esther's Courageous Stand
From Brokenness To Beauty Written By The Pen of Grace

The Ultimate Guide to Massive Action- From Plans to Reality
A Heart Of Conviction
Serving In The Shadows
Repentance Revealed The Road Back To God
The Chief Sinner Meets The Chief Saviour Reflections On I Timothy 1:15
Answer The Call - 31 Days of Biblical Action
The Birthmark of the Believer
Reflections on Calvary's Cross
The Kingdom Builder Paul's Bold Proclamation of Christ
The Animal Of Pride
The Reach That Restores Christ Love For The Broken
Paul- The Many Roles of a Servant of Christ
Unshakeable Faith- 31 Days of Peace in God's Word
O Come, Let Us Adore Him- A Christmas Devotional
The Shepherd's Voice
The Trail From Vision To Mission
Enabled- Living God's Purpose With Power
Held Back But Not Defeated
The Enoch Walk
The Power and Precision of God's Word
The Children Who Found Christmas
Hearts of Valor - Faithful in the Call
Why It Matters Finding Hope in Moments of Frustration
The Wild West Lives On McCall Family Adventures
Igniting Courage Fueling Your Heart To Serve The Lord
The Characters of Christmas
When Jealousy Takes Aim
Fan The Flame
Faith Comes By Hearing
Intentional Love A 31-Day Devotional on Courtship

The Anointing A Shepherd's Touch Of Grace
Unveiling God's Masterpiece The Indestructible Word of God
Heart Strings of Scripture
The War Cry Of A Conqueror
The Law of Accountability The Measure Of A Leader
The Law of Adaptability Thriving Through Change and Challenge
The Poetry Of Us

Dedication

To you, dear reader,

This book is for you—the dreamer, the believer, the one who knows that love is more than words on a page, more than fleeting moments or grand gestures. Love is found in the quiet spaces, in the everyday rhythms of life, in the hands that reach for each other even when the world feels heavy. Love is in the patience that listens, in the kindness that forgives, in the steady choice to stay, even when it would be easier to walk away.

This is for the ones who love fiercely, who give selflessly, and who cherish the beauty of a love that lasts. It is for those who understand that love is not about perfection but about presence. It is not measured by how loudly it is spoken but by how deeply it is felt. It is the warmth of a familiar embrace, the comfort of knowing you are seen, valued, and treasured—not for what you do but simply for who you are.

If you have ever loved and lost, if you have fought for love, if you have struggled to believe in love again, may these words remind you that love is always worth it. Love is poetry—not just in ink but in the way we choose to love, in the way we give of ourselves, in the way we hold on through the storms.

Wherever you are on your journey, may you find a reflection of your heart within these pages. May you be reminded that love is not just something we hope for—it is something we create, something we nurture, something we live. And in the end, love is not just a story—it is the most beautiful poetry ever written.

This is the poetry of us.

"Love is not merely spoken; it is lived. It is found in the quiet moments, the selfless gestures, the steady presence of a heart that chooses to stay. Love is the poetry we write—not with words alone, but with every act of kindness, every whisper of grace, and every moment we choose each other."

Introduction

Love is more than a fleeting feeling or a perfect moment captured in time—it is the poetry of life itself, written in the soft whispers of kindness, the steady rhythm of commitment, and the unshakable strength of two hearts entwined. "The Poetry of Us" is not just about grand romantic gestures, but about the gentle moments that make love lasting—the way a hand reaches for another in times of need, the way a quiet glance speaks a thousand words, and the way love grows even in the ordinary. Love is in the warmth of a shared laugh, in the patience that listens without judgment, and in the compassion that chooses to stay when things get hard. It is not just found in words, but in actions, in forgiveness, in understanding, and in the selfless decision to put another's heart before your own. Love is both delicate and powerful, strong enough to endure life's storms and tender enough to bring peace in the chaos. Like poetry, love is felt in the pauses as much as in the words, in the silences as much as in the declarations. It is a language of its own, woven through the moments we cherish and the memories we hold close. This book is a celebration of that love—the love that is deep, real, and beautifully imperfect. It is about the poetry that exists in everyday gestures, in quiet sacrifices, and in the steady, unwavering presence of someone who truly cares. Love is not just something we say; it is something we live, something we give, and something that shapes us in ways words alone cannot capture. This is the poetry of us—the story of love written not only in ink but in the way we love each other every single day.

Chapter 1 - The Language of Love

When words become the melody of the heart.

Love is more than just a word, more than a feeling, more than a moment—it is a language, a melody, a song that plays softly in the background of life, weaving its way into the hearts of those who truly listen. Love speaks in ways that do not always require sound, yet its voice is the strongest and most enduring of all. It is spoken in whispered prayers, in laughter shared between two people who know each other so well that they can communicate without speaking at all. It is found in the way someone's name is said with warmth and tenderness, in the steady reassurance of words like "I'm here," "I understand," and "You don't have to do this alone." The language of love is not just in poetry or in grand declarations, but in the quiet moments of kindness, in the way one heart reaches out to another without hesitation or expectation. It is in the way a mother's voice soothes a crying child in the middle of the night, in the way a friend says, "You are enough," when self-doubt begins to creep in, in the way a husband tells his wife, "You are beautiful," not because of how she looks, but because of who she is. Love's language is both simple and powerful, both familiar and endless, and it is understood by every person, no matter their background, no matter where they come from. It is not bound by a single tongue, nor is it confined to words at all. It is spoken in a comforting embrace, in a hand held tightly during times of uncertainty, in a small, thoughtful gesture that says, "I see you. I hear you. You matter." Love's voice is heard in the patience of someone who waits, in the compassion of someone who forgives, in the encouragement of someone who believes in you when you have stopped believing in yourself. It is the soft melody that plays in the background of life's hardest days, reminding us that we are not alone, that there is still light, that there is still hope. Love is a language that can be spoken by anyone, in any place, at any time, and yet it is never exhausted, never drained, never diminished by overuse. It only grows stronger the more it is shared. The language of love is not in perfect words, but in honest ones. It is in the brave admissions of "I was wrong," "I forgive you," "I love you anyway." It is in the apologies that heal wounds, in the promises that are kept even when they are difficult to hold onto, in the vows that are whispered again and again, long after they were first spoken. Love is not found in empty words, but in words that carry weight, in words that have meaning, in words that are backed by action. It is in the quiet "good morning" messages that make someone feel thought of, in the handwritten note left on a pillow, in the phone call made just to check in. It is in the way a father tells his daughter, "I'm proud of you," in the way a sister reassures her brother, "I'll always have your back." Love's language is not always loud, but it is always present, always speaking, always filling the spaces between us with its gentle, unwavering melody. It is the song that never fades, the voice that never silences, the words that, once spoken, live on forever in the heart of the one who hears them. The language of love is the only language that needs no translation, for it is felt before it is understood, known before it is learned. It is the first language we hear when we enter this world, the one that comforts us in childhood, that strengthens us in adulthood, that carries us through every season of life. It is spoken in every goodbye that carries the hope of a reunion, in every "be safe" whispered as someone leaves, in every "I love you" that is said, whether it is returned or not. Love does not demand to be acknowledged; it simply exists, quietly, faithfully, unconditionally. And perhaps that is its greatest power—not in the way it is spoken, but in the way it is felt, in the way it remains, in the way it never leaves those who have known its melody. The language of love is the most beautiful song ever written, and it is a song that never truly ends.

Chapter 2 - Handwritten in Forever

The beauty of love penned in time.

Love is not just a fleeting feeling or a temporary moment of happiness. It is something far deeper, something that stretches beyond time, something that lasts even when the years change and life takes unexpected turns. Love is handwritten in forever, etched into the story of our lives, written on the pages of our hearts in ink that never fades. It is found in the letters we never throw away and in the notes scribbled in the margins of a book given by someone dear. Love lingers in the words whispered in quiet moments, staying with us long after they are spoken.

It is seen in the way two people remember the same day differently, yet cherish the emotions just the same. It exists in the way a simple phrase can transport someone back to a memory so vivid it feels as if no time has passed at all. Love is the poetry of time, the handwriting of the heart, and the script of moments that define us in ways we never fully realize while we are living them. It is written in the way hands reach for each other instinctively and in the way eyes meet across a crowded room, speaking without words. Love is heard in the warmth of a familiar name, spoken as if it is the most precious sound in the world.

True love does not fade with time; instead, it deepens and grows richer with every moment shared, every challenge faced, and every quiet night spent together. It remains steady in the comfort of knowing that even when everything else changes, love stays. The beauty of love is not measured by grand gestures or extravagant declarations. It is found in the small things, in the notes left on the kitchen counter, in the inside jokes that have lasted for years, and in the little traditions that have become sacred without ever being planned.

Love is present in the prayers whispered over a sleeping child. It is visible in the gentle way an elderly couple still holds hands, a gesture that speaks of a lifetime spent together. It is felt in a letter from a loved one, read over and over again because each word carries the weight of eternity. Love is written in time, not only in the moments we cherish but also in the spaces in between—the waiting, the growing, the learning to love more deeply than we ever thought possible.

It is found in the strength to stay, in the grace to forgive, in the patience to endure, and in the courage to keep writing the story together even when life is difficult. Love is the ink that never runs dry, the handwriting that never fades, and the message that never loses its meaning, no matter how many years pass. It is written in vows whispered beneath the sky and in letters folded and kept safe in a box. Love is sealed with quiet determination rather than loud declarations.

It is not a fleeting moment but a collection of moments strung together like pearls on a string. Each one builds upon the last, making the story more beautiful. Love is the reason poetry is written, the reason songs are sung, and the reason stories are told again and again. Love is not just something to be felt; it is something to be remembered, something to be shared, and something to be kept close to the heart.

It is the reason a child clings to bedtime stories whispered in the soft glow of a nightlight. It is why a letter written decades ago still brings tears to the eyes of the one who reads it. It is why a simple "I love you" spoken at the right moment can change everything. Love is the kind of thing that cannot be erased, even when distance separates, even when time moves forward, even when the world changes. It remains because true love does not live only in the moment—it is handwritten in forever.

Love is seen in the way a mother traces her child's face with her fingers, as if memorizing every detail. It is in the way a soldier keeps a worn picture of home tucked inside his pocket. It is in the way two people can sit in silence and still feel completely understood. Love is a language that never needs translation, a story that never loses its meaning, and a truth that is written so deeply in the soul that nothing can take it away.

It is the reason why some songs never grow old, why certain words are never forgotten, and why love letters from long ago still make hearts race. Love is found in the way a grandparent tells the story of how they met their love, as if time has not dulled the memory, as if the moment is still alive in their heart. It is not just a passing emotion or something that comes and goes. Love is permanent, lingering in the spaces between now and forever.

It is the reason a single touch can bring back a thousand memories and why a familiar scent can transport someone back in time. It is why the heart knows what the mind may forget. Love is the gentle echo of a life well-lived and the quiet reminder that what is truly cherished is never lost. It is written in the way a person waits for someone they love and in the way faith holds on even when the road is long.

It is in the way two people choose each other again and again, no matter how much time has passed. Love is in the way hands stay clasped through the years and in the way promises are kept long after they are made. It is in the whispered "I will always love you," which is not just a momentary feeling but a vow written in the fabric of forever. Love is the letter that is never thrown away, the words that never fade, and the poetry that never stops being written.

It is the script of every moment that matters, the ink of every memory worth holding onto, and the handwriting of the soul that continues to write its story even after the last page is turned. Love does not end when life changes—it simply finds new ways to be written, new chapters to unfold, and new melodies to be sung. It is the kind of thing that lasts, not because time stands still, but because love does not need time to exist.

Love is timeless, infinite, and written beyond the reach of the clock. It exists beyond the grasp of the years and beyond the limits of what can be measured. It is handwritten in forever because love, when it is true, when it is deep, and when it is real, is never lost. It only grows, strengthens, and continues, forever written in the hearts of those who have known its beauty. It is forever etched in the spaces where love once was.

Love is forever inscribed in the story of those who dared to love with their whole heart. It is not something we leave behind; it is something we carry forward. It is something we pass down and something we write in the lives of those we touch. Love is, and always will be, the most beautiful story ever told, the most precious letter ever written, and the most lasting promise ever spoken. It is, and always will be, handwritten in forever.

Chapter 3 - Every Line, Every Look

How unspoken moments create the deepest poetry.

Love is not always spoken in words, yet it is still heard in the silence between heartbeats, in the spaces between sentences, and in the quiet moments where two souls simply exist together. The deepest expressions of love are often not found in grand speeches or carefully written letters but in the unspoken exchanges that pass between two people who truly understand each other. Every glance, every sigh, and every moment of quiet companionship tells a story that no words could fully capture.

Love is written in the way eyes meet across a crowded room and recognize something familiar, something safe, and something that speaks louder than a thousand conversations. It is in the way one person reaches instinctively for another's hand when crossing the street. It is present in the way a simple touch on the shoulder communicates reassurance. Love is found in the way a comforting presence can calm an anxious heart without a single word being spoken.

Some of the most meaningful conversations happen without sound. They occur in the stolen glances, in the shared smiles, and in the soft sigh of relief when someone you love is near. Love is written not just in ink on paper but in the way someone looks at another as if they are the most beautiful thing they have ever seen. It is found in the way someone's expression softens at the mere mention of a name. It is seen in the way two people who have been together for years can communicate with nothing more than a look.

The poetry of love is woven into the way a mother watches her child sleep. It is reflected in the way a father places a protective hand on his son's shoulder. It is present in the way an elderly couple sits side by side in peaceful silence, knowing that words are not always necessary when love has been spoken for a lifetime in every touch, every glance, and every moment of simply being together.

Love is not just in what is said but in what is felt. It is in the way someone lingers in a doorway before leaving, in the way they turn back for one last look, and in the way they remember the smallest details about the person they love. Love exists in the memory of a favorite song, in the way someone takes their coffee, and in the stories that make them laugh even when they have heard them a hundred times before.

Love is in the way someone reaches for another in the dark. It is in the way they pull a blanket over them while they sleep. It is in the way they instinctively know when the other person is hurting, even when no words have been spoken. The deepest poetry of love is found in the moments most people overlook. It is in the pauses, in the unspoken promises, and in the way one person stays when it would have been easier to walk away.

Love is found in the way someone listens—not just with their ears but with their heart. It is reflected in the way they hold onto the things left unsaid and in the way they remember the words that were too difficult to speak. Love is seen in the way someone pulls another into an embrace at just the right moment.

It is in the way they give space when they know it is needed. It is present in the way they sit quietly beside someone who just needs to know they are not alone.

Love is in the way someone waits. It is in the way they stand by another's side without question. It is in the way they show up, time and time again, not because they have to but because they want to. Love is in the way a hand brushes a strand of hair behind an ear. It is in the way a forehead is pressed against another in a silent exchange of strength. It is in the way someone squeezes a hand just a little tighter when they know the other person is struggling.

Love is in the way someone watches another walk away and silently prays they will return safely. It is in the way someone holds another just a little longer when they know they are about to say goodbye. Love is in the details. It is in the moments that seem small but are actually everything.

Love is in the way someone turns up the volume on their partner's favorite song without being asked. It is in the way they save the last bite of dessert for them. It is in the way they make sure their loved one's car is warmed up on a cold morning. Love is in the way someone sits beside another in silence, knowing that words are not always needed to bring comfort.

Love is in the way someone notices the tiredness in another's eyes and quietly takes something off their plate, offering help without making a big deal about it. It is in the way someone looks at another as if they are still seeing them for the first time, even after years have passed. Love is in the way someone instinctively protects another. It is in the way they stand up for them even when they are not there to hear it. It is in the way they believe in them even when they struggle to believe in themselves.

Love is in the way someone forgives. It is in the way they choose to stay. It is in the way they keep showing up even on the hardest days. Love is in the way someone notices when another is about to cry. It is in the way they do not ask questions but simply pull them close. It is in the way someone reaches for another in their sleep, unconsciously searching for the warmth of their presence.

Love is in the way someone memorizes the details of another's face. It is in the way they trace the lines of their features as if trying to hold onto time itself. It is in the way someone holds another's hand a little tighter when they are afraid. It is in the way they lean into their touch when they need reassurance. It is in the way they simply exist together, breathing in the same space, hearts beating in quiet harmony.

The deepest poetry of love is not always written with words. It is felt in the quiet, unnoticed moments. It is found in the small gestures. It is seen in the way someone makes another feel safe without ever needing to say a thing.

Love is in the way someone catches another's eye from across the room and instantly understands what they are thinking. It is in the way someone stays up late just to listen. It is in the way they drop everything when the person they love needs them. Love is not always about what is spoken but about what is known. It is about being seen, being understood, and being held in the silent spaces where words do not need to exist.

Love is about the way someone feels at home in another's presence. It is about the way two hearts can speak the same language without saying a single thing. Love is in the way someone's eyes soften when they see another after a long day.

It is in the way they instinctively move closer, as if drawn by something beyond words.

Love is in the way someone stays when life gets hard. It is in the way they choose to keep loving even when it is not easy. Love is found in the quiet moments, in the pauses, and in the spaces where words are not needed. It is in the way someone's heart skips a beat when they realize they are looking at the person they never want to live without.

Love is in the way someone places their hand over another's, silently letting them know that whatever happens, they are not alone. Love is written in every glance, in every touch, and in every quiet moment of understanding. It is not just found in words. It is found in the poetry of unspoken moments, in the silent exchanges, and in the knowing looks.

Love is in the simple, undeniable truth that it does not always need to be said out loud to be heard.

Chapter 4 - Ink-Stained Promises

Commitments written on the heart, not just on paper.

Promises are more than words spoken in a moment. They are more than ink on a page, more than vows exchanged in front of witnesses, more than neatly written letters sealed with affection. Promises are the heart's way of saying, "I will be here. I will not leave. I will not forget." They are not meant to fade with time or change with circumstances. They are meant to endure, to hold strong, to remain even when everything else shifts. True promises are written not just in ink but in the heart, where they cannot be erased by distance, by hardship, or by the storms of life. A real promise is not just a phrase whispered in joy or spoken when the sun is shining—it is something that still holds meaning when the skies grow dark, when the days feel heavy, when the road is uncertain. It is in the way someone stays when they could have walked away, in the way they hold on even when life pulls them in different directions, in the way they choose love again and again, even when it would be easier to give up. A true promise is not written with fleeting emotions but with deep, unwavering devotion. It is found in the way a parent never stops loving their child, no matter how many mistakes are made. It is seen in the way a friend shows up, time and time again, refusing to let silence or distance break the bond that was built over years of laughter, tears, and shared memories. It is felt in the way a spouse reaches for their partner's hand, not just on the wedding day, but decades later, when life has tested every vow spoken in youth. Promises are the foundation of trust, the steady ground beneath the fragile weight of human hearts. They are not just words; they are commitments that shape the way we love, the way we forgive, the way we hold onto the people who mean the most. A promise is saying, "I will walk with you through the storms. I will stand beside you when the world turns against you. I will believe in you, even on the days you do not believe in yourself." True promises do not depend on convenience. They do not crumble when life becomes difficult. They do not disappear when feelings fade or when time stretches the spaces between two souls. Instead, they are carved deep, woven into the very fabric of who we are, binding hearts together with invisible threads that do not break. A real promise is not measured in words but in actions. It is in the way someone stays up late to listen, even when they are exhausted. It is in the way they choose patience over anger, understanding over judgment, love over resentment. It is in the way they fight for someone they love, even when it is difficult, even when every reason to walk away seems justified. Love is not just in the easy moments, in the laughter, in the sunshine—it is in the battles, in the forgiveness, in the quiet choices to hold on when everything says to let go. Promises are written in the way someone whispers "I'm not going anywhere" and then proves it, again and again. They are in the way a father shows up to every game, every recital, every important moment, no matter how busy life becomes. They are in the way a mother listens, truly listens, even when the words spoken are difficult to hear. They are in the way a friend refuses to leave, even when mistakes have been made. They are in the way a husband holds his wife's hand in the hospital room, in the way a wife stands beside her husband when life takes everything from them but love. Promises are not just spoken; they are lived. They are written in the way a person sacrifices their own comfort to make someone else feel safe, in the way they offer grace when they have every right to walk away, in the way they hold on to love when time and trials attempt to wear it down. True promises are not made of fragile ink but of something stronger, something unbreakable, something eternal. They are written in the way someone prays for another, in the way they whisper their name in the quiet moments of the night, in the way they hope for them even when hope seems small. They are in the way someone fights for another's dreams as if they were their own. They are in the way someone says, "I believe in you," and means it with every part of their soul. A true promise does not fade with time. It does not lose its meaning when difficulties arise. It is as strong in the storms as it was in the sunlight. It is something that cannot be taken back, cannot be undone, cannot be replaced by something easier. It is a vow that stands, even when life changes everything else. Promises are not just spoken between lovers, but between friends who have walked through fire together, between siblings who have stood side by side since childhood, between parents and children who have carried each other through seasons of joy and sorrow. A promise is not just for today—it is for tomorrow, for the next year, for the lifetime that stretches ahead, unknown but held together by love. It is in the way someone says, "You are not alone," and proves it in the way they stay. It is in the way someone keeps showing up, keeps holding on, keeps loving without condition. A promise is not in the perfection of never failing, never making mistakes, never falling short—it is in the willingness to get back up, to try again, to fight for what matters, even when it is hard. It is in the way someone chooses to love, even on the days when love feels like a choice instead of a feeling. Promises are in the way someone leaves the light on, just in case the person they love decides to come home. They are in the way someone waits, no matter how long it takes. They are in the way someone remembers the little things—the way someone loves flowers but not roses, the way they take their coffee, the way their eyes light up when they talk about their dreams. A true promise is not just about loyalty; it is about love so deep that it writes itself into the fabric of another person's soul. It is about loving someone enough to stay, enough to forgive, enough to see past the hard moments and into the heart that is worth fighting for. It is about knowing that love is not about perfection but about perseverance. It is about standing beside someone, hand in hand, through the best and the worst, through the joys and the struggles, through the moments that define what true love really is. Promises are written in the way someone holds onto another, in the way they refuse to let go, in the way they whisper, "I will love you for all of my days." They are in the way love stands firm, even when time tests it, even when the world tries to break it apart. Ink may fade, but a promise written on the heart does not. It stays. It remains. It endures. It is written not just for today, not just for tomorrow, but for forever. And that is the kind of love that never dies.

Chapter 5 - Rhymes of the Heart

How love flows in perfect harmony.

Love is like a song, a melody that plays in the background of life, shaping every moment with its quiet rhythm, moving like poetry written not with ink but with the beating of two hearts that somehow find each other in a world full of noise. It is the steady hum of devotion, the soft whisper of kindness, the harmony between two souls that seem to understand each other without effort, as if they have always been meant to dance to the same tune. Love flows like a river, winding through the seasons of life, sometimes gentle, sometimes rushing, but always finding its way forward, always shaping the landscape of the hearts it touches. It does not demand to be heard but makes itself known in the way one person instinctively reaches for another's hand, in the way laughter intertwines like notes in a song, in the way silence feels full instead of empty when two people truly belong to one another. Love is found in the rhythm of shared moments, in the simple joys of daily life, in the way one person knows when the other needs comfort without needing to ask. It is in the way a mother hums a lullaby to her child, the sound wrapping around them like a warm embrace. It is in the way a father's voice carries strength, even in the quietest words of reassurance. It is in the way friends laugh together, their joy blending like a perfect chorus. It is in the way lovers move in sync, their hearts speaking a language only they can understand. Love is the song that does not need words to be understood, the poetry that does not need paper to be remembered, the music that lingers long after the moment has passed. It is in the way a glance carries the weight of a thousand emotions, in the way a heartbeat quickens at the sound of a familiar voice, in the way a gentle touch can calm an anxious soul. Love does not rush; it moves at its own pace, unhurried, steady, always present, always singing. It is the echo of kindness left in the wake of a thoughtful act, the steady beat of faithfulness in a world that too often forgets how to stay. Love is the harmony between two people who choose each other, again and again, no matter how many notes life plays between them. It is in the way one person stays awake just to listen to another's dreams, in the way they remember the little things—the way they like their coffee, the stories that make them laugh, the song that brings tears to their eyes. It is in the way someone waits at the door just to watch the person they love walk inside safely. It is in the way someone holds another's hand a little tighter when they are scared, in the way someone leans their head on another's shoulder just because they feel at home there. Love is not perfect, but it is always in motion, always growing, always finding new ways to be expressed. It is in the quiet moments, in the soft exchanges, in the rhythm of two hearts learning to beat in sync even when life pulls them in different directions. It is in the way someone whispers "I love you" not just with words but with actions—with patience, with sacrifice, with the choice to stay even when things are difficult. Love is in the way a mother holds her child long after they have fallen asleep, not wanting to let go of the moment. It is in the way a father watches his daughter from across the room, his heart swelling with pride at the person she is becoming. It is in the way an old couple walks together, their steps slow but steady, their love written in the wrinkles of their hands, in the familiar comfort of a love that has stood the test of time. Love is a song that never truly ends; it simply finds new verses, new harmonies, new ways to be sung. It is in the way two people sit together in silence and still feel completely understood. It is in the way a hug lingers just a second longer than necessary, in the way a smile speaks louder than words ever could. It is in the way someone makes a space for another in their life, not just in the good times, but in the hard ones, in the uncertain ones, in the moments that require patience and faith. Love is not just in the grand gestures, but in the simple, steady rhythm of choosing each other every day. It is in the way someone waits, in the way they forgive, in the way they hold onto hope even when life has made it difficult. Love is the melody that weaves through the seasons, the song that plays even when the world is quiet. It is the way one person knows exactly what to say to bring peace to another's heart, the way a single word can bring comfort, the way the presence of someone we love can turn the ordinary into something extraordinary. Love is in the way someone leaves a note on the counter just to say "I was thinking of you." It is in the way someone makes sure another has everything they need before thinking of themselves. It is in the way someone whispers "I'm proud of you" when they know the other person needs to hear it. Love is in the small moments, in the spaces between conversations, in the way one soul aligns with another and creates something that cannot be explained, only felt. It is in the way one person's laughter becomes another's favorite sound, in the way memories are woven into the fabric of life like lyrics to a song that is never forgotten. It is in the way someone says "be safe" instead of "goodbye," in the way they hold on a little longer when they hug, in the way they always show up, no matter how much time has passed. Love is a song that never fades, a melody that lingers even when the people who sang it are far apart. It is the rhythm of life, the steady beat of devotion, the quiet music of two hearts that refuse to let go. It is in the way someone saves the last bite of food for the person they love. It is in the way someone takes the time to make another's favorite meal, even on a busy day. It is in the way someone prays for another without them ever knowing. Love is in the unspoken moments, in the harmony of two people who may not always have the perfect words but always have the perfect understanding. It is in the way someone looks at another as if they are the most precious thing they have ever seen, in the way a familiar hand feels like home, in the way love does not need to be loud to be strong. It is in the way someone fights for another's dreams as if they were their own. It is in the way they believe in each other, in the way they hold on, in the way they create something beautiful out of the simple act of loving and being loved. Love is not something that happens all at once; it is something that grows, something that deepens, something that finds its way into the smallest corners of life and fills them with meaning. It is in the way someone stays, in the way they choose to love even on the days when it is not easy. It is in the way someone listens, in the way they remember, in the way they make room for another in their life. Love is the song that never stops playing, the poetry that never stops being written, the heartbeat that never stops keeping time with another. It is the harmony of two lives woven together, the gentle refrain of something that is meant to last. It is the way one soul finds another and says, "This is home." Love is the song, the rhythm, the rhyme of the heart, flowing in perfect harmony, forever written in the melodies of time.

Chapter 6 - The Softest Verse

Compassion in the quietest moments of love.

Love does not always announce itself with grand gestures or loud declarations. Sometimes, it is found in the smallest, softest moments—ones so quiet that they could be overlooked by anyone who is not paying attention. Love is not always about saying the right thing at the right time, but about knowing when words are not needed at all. It is in the way a person sits beside someone who is grieving, offering nothing but their presence because they know that sometimes the greatest comfort is not in speaking, but in simply being there. It is in the way a mother gently strokes her child's hair while they sleep, as if memorizing every detail, knowing these quiet moments are precious and fleeting. It is in the way a father watches his child from across the room, his heart swelling with pride, even if he does not say a word. Love is the hand that reaches out instinctively in the dark, the warmth of a touch that speaks of safety and belonging, the deep breath of relief when someone walks through the door after being gone for too long. It is in the way someone notices when another person is tired and offers them a moment of rest without making them feel weak for needing it. It is in the way someone listens, truly listens, not just to the words being spoken, but to the emotions behind them, to the silent cries hidden between sentences, to the things left unsaid. Love is the whisper of reassurance in the middle of the night, the steady heartbeat that reminds you that you are not alone, the way someone covers another with a blanket when they have fallen asleep without realizing it. It is in the way someone makes sure another has enough to eat, in the way they remember little details about their favorite things, in the way they do not hesitate to step in when life feels too heavy to carry alone. Love does not always need to be spoken to be understood. It is in the way someone waits for another to be ready, in the way they give space without making it feel like distance, in the way they are patient when the other needs time to heal. It is in the way someone picks up on the tiny changes that no one else would notice, in the way they recognize sadness in a voice that is trying too hard to sound okay, in the way they do not ask for explanations but simply offer understanding. Love is the willingness to sit in silence with someone who is struggling, to let them know that their pain is seen, that they do not have to face it alone. It is in the way someone wipes away a tear before it even falls, in the way they instinctively pull another into a hug at just the right moment, in the way they know when to let go and when to hold on tighter. The softest verse of love is written in the spaces between words, in the moments that do not need to be announced, in the quiet exchanges that hold more weight than any speech ever could. It is in the way someone smiles at another from across the room, in the way their eyes light up at the sight of the one they love, in the way their presence alone is enough to make everything feel a little bit lighter. Love is in the way someone makes another feel safe enough to let down their guard, in the way they become a place of refuge without even trying. It is in the gentle way someone tucks a strand of hair behind another's ear, in the way they trace patterns absentmindedly on their skin, in the way their fingers interlock without a second thought, as if their hands were meant to find each other. Love is found in the pauses, in the moments when two people are simply existing together, wrapped in the comfort of knowing that they are loved, that they are seen, that they belong. It is in the way someone makes an effort, even when they do not have to, in the way they remember the things that others might forget, in the way they choose kindness when it would be easier to walk away. It is in the way someone whispers, "I'm here," and actually means it, in the way they show up without being asked, in the way they stay even when things are difficult. Love is not just in the grand gestures; it is in the quiet, consistent presence of someone who cares. It is in the way a person lets another go ahead in line, in the way they stop to check on someone who looks like they are having a hard day, in the way they offer their seat to a stranger without thinking twice. It is in the way someone recognizes when another needs a moment to breathe and gives it to them without making them feel guilty. Love is in the way a person sacrifices their own comfort for another's peace, in the way they put someone else's happiness above their own, not out of obligation, but because they truly want to. It is in the way they notice when someone is trying to be strong but needs permission to fall apart. It is in the way they hold them without judgment, in the way they make space for their pain without rushing them to move on. Love is in the way someone speaks gently even when they are upset, in the way they choose to be kind even when they have every reason to be angry, in the way they forgive even when they have been hurt. It is in the way someone stands up for another, in the way they protect them not just from the world, but from their own self-doubt. It is in the way they believe in them when they cannot believe in themselves. Love is in the way someone's voice softens when they say a name that means something to them, in the way their hands tremble slightly when they are holding something precious, in the way their heartbeat slows when they are near the person who feels like home. It is in the way someone carries another's burdens without making them feel like a burden at all, in the way they share their strength without expecting anything in return. Love is found in the gentle patience of waiting for someone to be ready, in the quiet understanding of knowing that healing takes time. It is in the way someone reaches for another in the middle of the night, needing nothing more than to feel their warmth. It is in the way someone lingers in an embrace just a second longer than necessary, in the way they turn back for one last look before leaving, in the way they stay up just to make sure the other falls asleep first. Love is in the soft moments, in the spaces where words fail, in the kindness that is given without expectation. It is in the way someone holds another's hand under the table, in the way they trace absentminded circles on their skin, in the way they do not hesitate to pull them close when they sense their sadness. Love is in the way someone notices the way another's voice changes when they are tired, in the way they learn every little habit and love them all the same, in the way they cherish the things that make the other person unique. It is in the way someone whispers "You're safe," in the way they show up before being asked, in the way they stay long after everyone else has left. The softest verse of love is not found in loud, dramatic expressions, but in the quiet acts of compassion, in the moments where one person reminds another that they are not alone. It is in the way someone saves the last bite of food without mentioning it, in the way they let another take the last blanket, in the way they adjust their steps to match the pace of the one walking beside them. Love is in the way someone tucks a note into a pocket for another to find later, in the way they gently squeeze a hand in passing, in the way they make sure another always has a place at their table. It is in the way someone gives their time, their patience, their kindness, simply because they care. Love is not just about saying the right words; it is about being there in the moments when words are not enough. It is about choosing to be gentle when the world is harsh, about choosing to love when it would be easier to walk away, about choosing kindness even when no one is watching. Love is the softest verse in the song of life, the quiet harmony that holds everything together, the unspoken promise that says, "I see you, I hear you, I love you." And sometimes, the softest verse is the one that speaks the loudest of all.

Chapter 7 - In the Margins of Our Story

The little things that make love profound.

Love is not always written in bold letters or declared in grand, sweeping gestures; instead, it is often found in the quiet, unnoticed moments, in the margins of our story, where the little things live. It is in the way one person remembers how another takes their coffee, in the way they save the last bite of dessert because they know it is the other's favorite, in the way they instinctively reach for their hand in a crowded place as if to say, "You are safe with me." Love is in the way someone stops what they are doing to really listen, in the way they take a deep breath instead of raising their voice, in the way they choose kindness when frustration would be easier. It is in the gentle way someone brushes a strand of hair behind another's ear, in the way they tuck a blanket around them when they have fallen asleep, in the way they press a kiss to their forehead, not because they have to, but because they cannot help but show how much they care. Love is in the way two people sit in silence, completely comfortable, knowing that their presence is enough. It is in the way one person notices when the other is struggling, in the way they sense when laughter is forced, in the way they ask, "Are you okay?" and really mean it. It is found in the way they linger in an embrace, just a second longer than necessary, as if holding onto time itself. Love is in the way someone makes space for another, not just in their home, but in their life, in their plans, in their heart. It is in the way they leave a note on the counter just to say, "Have a good day." It is in the way they remember the little details that no one else would—how they prefer the window seat, how they always tap their fingers to a certain rhythm, how they get quiet when they are overwhelmed. Love is in the way someone recognizes the things that make another person who they are, in the way they see them fully and love them just as they are, without expectation or condition. It is in the way someone instinctively stands a little closer when they sense the other is uncomfortable, in the way they check the weather before they leave just to remind them to take a jacket, in the way they squeeze their hand three times as a silent way of saying, "I love you." Love is in the way one person notices when another is tired and makes sure they get a moment to rest, in the way they take on the little burdens without making a big deal out of it, in the way they see the weight the other carries and do their best to lighten it. It is in the way someone stops by the store just to pick up their favorite snack, in the way they text, "Let me know when you get home," because their heart would not rest until they know they are safe. It is in the way they show up, not just in the good times, but in the hard ones, in the messy ones, in the moments when life feels overwhelming and all they can offer is their presence—but somehow, that is enough. Love is in the way someone instinctively knows when the other needs comfort, in the way they wrap their arms around them before they even ask, in the way they know when to speak and when to simply hold them. It is in the way they make the other person feel seen, heard, understood, even on the days when they do not have the right words. It is in the way someone remembers things that even the person themselves has forgotten, in the way they bring up a childhood memory, a dream once shared, a moment that felt small but somehow mattered. Love is in the way someone notices the books left unfinished on their nightstand, in the way they hum along to the same song they have played a thousand times, in the way they hold onto old letters and photographs because they know that some moments are too precious to let go. It is in the way they hold hands under the table, in the way they trace circles on their skin absentmindedly, in the way they smile at them like they are the most beautiful thing they have ever seen, even when they do not feel beautiful at all. Love is in the way someone instinctively knows when the other needs space and when they need to be held. It is in the way they remember which foods make them sick, in the way they pull them closer when they are having a bad dream, in the way they stay up late just to listen when something is weighing heavy on their heart. It is in the way they remember to take a picture because they know that one day, this moment will be a memory they will want to hold onto. It is in the way they tuck their own needs away for a moment, just to make sure the other person is okay. It is in the way they wait, in the way they forgive, in the way they show up time and time again, even when life makes it difficult. Love is in the small gestures, in the unnoticed moments, in the in-between spaces that no one else sees. It is in the way someone gently tilts the other's chin up when they are feeling defeated, in the way they brush their fingers across their back absentmindedly, in the way they pull them closer in the middle of the night. It is in the way they learn to love not just the easy parts, but the complicated, messy, imperfect parts as well. Love is in the way someone leaves the light on a little longer because they know the other does not like the dark, in the way they turn the volume down when they are sleeping, in the way they instinctively reach for their hand when they cross the street. It is in the way they whisper, "I'm proud of you," even when the other person does not feel worthy of praise. It is in the way they stand up for them, even when they are not there to hear it. It is in the way they make them feel safe enough to be their true self, without fear of judgment. It is in the way they notice the little changes—the way their voice sounds when they are tired, the way their laughter fades when something is bothering them, the way their shoulders tense when they are overwhelmed. Love is in the way someone says, "I love you," not just with words, but with actions, with presence, with the unshaken commitment to be there in ways that truly matter. It is in the way someone chooses another, every single day, in the way they hold onto them even when life tries to pull them apart. It is in the way they make the smallest moments feel like the biggest ones. Love is in the way someone lingers a little longer when they hug, in the way they turn back for one last glance before leaving, in the way they remember the details that make another person feel cherished. It is in the way they notice, in the way they care, in the way they love not just in the big moments, but in the quiet, unspoken ones—the ones that happen in the margins of the story, the ones that may not always be written down, but are always, always felt.

Chapter 8 - When Love Speaks in Whispers

Gentle expressions that echo forever.

Love is not always loud. It does not always arrive with grand declarations or dramatic displays. More often, it is found in the softest moments, in the quiet gestures that seem small but leave an imprint on the heart that never fades. Love speaks in whispers, in the gentle way one person reaches for another's hand without needing a reason, in the way a mother hums a lullaby long after her child has fallen asleep, in the way a father places a steady hand on his child's shoulder as if to say, "I am here." Love is in the way someone pulls a blanket over another in the middle of the night, in the way they touch their arm gently when they sense something is wrong, in the way they wait at the door just to make sure their loved one arrives home safely. It is in the way they remember the little things—their favorite song, the way they like their coffee, the stories that bring light to their eyes. It is in the way they whisper "be safe" instead of "goodbye," in the way they send a message just to say "I'm thinking of you," in the way they choose kindness even when words are hard to find. Love is in the way someone notices the slight change in another's voice when they are sad, in the way they reach for them in the quiet moments, in the way they give their time without asking for anything in return. It is in the way someone stays up late just to listen, in the way they sit beside someone who is hurting, offering no advice, no solutions, just the comfort of presence. Love is in the way someone whispers, "I'm proud of you," even when the other person does not feel worthy of praise. It is in the way they carry the weight of another's burdens, not because they have to, but because love makes them want to. It is in the way they say, "I understand," when no one else does, in the way they forgive before the words "I'm sorry" are even spoken, in the way they see someone for who they truly are and love them just the same. Love is in the way someone reaches for another in their sleep, unconsciously searching for the warmth of their presence. It is in the way they sit beside them in silence, speaking volumes with nothing more than the steady rhythm of their breathing. It is in the way they brush their fingers across their hand absentmindedly, in the way they tuck a loose strand of hair behind their ear, in the way they press a gentle kiss to their forehead as if sealing a promise without ever speaking a word. Love is in the way someone whispers, "I will always be here," not just once, not just when it is easy, but over and over again, proving with their actions that those words are not just spoken but lived. It is in the way they instinctively know when to hold on and when to give space, in the way they sense what is needed before it is asked. It is in the way they whisper "You don't have to carry this alone," in the way they sit with someone through their fears, in the way they remain steady when everything else feels uncertain. Love is in the way someone lingers in an embrace, in the way they squeeze a hand just a little tighter, in the way they stay just a little longer because they know leaving would feel too soon. It is in the way they whisper, "You are enough," in the way they encourage, in the way they believe in someone even on the days they struggle to believe in themselves. It is in the way someone leaves a note tucked inside a pocket for another to find later, in the way they save the last piece of dessert without saying anything, in the way they make room for another in their life, not just in the good moments, but in the hard ones, in the messy ones, in the ones where love is tested and still chooses to stay. Love is in the way someone whispers a prayer over another as they sleep, in the way they place a protective hand on their back in a crowded place, in the way they instinctively shield them from the rain even if it means getting wet themselves. It is in the way someone whispers, "I see you," in the way they validate feelings that others dismiss, in the way they create a safe place for vulnerability to exist without fear. It is in the way someone whispers, "Take your time," in the way they are patient with healing, in the way they offer grace even when it is undeserved. It is in the way someone chooses to love quietly, steadily, consistently, proving over and over again that love is not just found in the loud moments, but in the whispers that echo forever. It is in the way someone turns back for one last glance, in the way they whisper, "Drive safe," as if those words alone can protect the one they love. It is in the way someone picks up on the things left unsaid, in the way they recognize when another is struggling even before they admit it. It is in the way someone lingers just a second longer before letting go, in the way they softly say "I love you" in passing, not as an afterthought, but as a habit, as a way of making sure those words never go unspoken. It is in the way someone whispers reassurance in moments of doubt, in the way they hold another's face in their hands and remind them of their worth, in the way they make love feel like a safe place to return to, always. Love is in the way someone memorizes another's face, as if afraid time will take away what they want to remember forever. It is in the way they protect without controlling, in the way they guide without forcing, in the way they love without expectation. It is in the way someone whispers, "I'm here," in the way they show up, in the way they stand beside another through every season, through every uncertainty, through every moment that life throws their way. Love is not just found in loud expressions of devotion but in the gentle, steady presence of someone who truly cares. It is in the way someone tucks their arm around another's shoulders on a cold night, in the way they stay up just to watch them sleep, in the way they remember the little things that no one else notices. Love is in the way someone picks up on the hesitation in another's voice, in the way they notice when laughter does not quite reach their eyes, in the way they whisper, "It's okay, you can tell me," and actually mean it. It is in the way someone whispers, "I've got you," in the way they wipe away tears before they fall, in the way they make the world feel softer just by being in it. Love is in the way someone slows their steps to match another's pace, in the way they offer their coat without being asked, in the way they notice when another needs a moment to breathe. It is in the way someone whispers encouragement in the middle of a storm, in the way they become a steady presence when life feels uncertain, in the way they bring warmth to the coldest moments. Love is in the whispers that do not fade, in the quiet words that stay long after they are spoken, in the moments that may seem small but hold the weight of eternity. It is in the way someone whispers, "You are loved," and means it, in the way they make love feel like something unshakable, something enduring, something that does not need to shout to be heard. Love is in the way someone's presence alone is enough, in the way they remind another, over and over again, that they are never alone. And perhaps, in the end, love is not just found in the words that are spoken loudly, but in the quietest whispers that stay with us forever.

Chapter 9 - Stanzas of Strength

Love that carries us through trials and triumphs.

Love is not only found in the lighthearted moments, in the easy days filled with laughter and warmth; it is also found in the storms, in the struggles, in the times when everything feels heavy, and yet, love stands strong. True love is not just a fleeting feeling that exists only when life is simple; it is a force that carries us when we are too weak to walk on our own. It is in the quiet way someone stays, not just when things are joyful, but when everything seems to be falling apart. It is in the way they reach for another's hand when fear takes over, in the way they whisper, "We will get through this," and mean it with every part of their soul. Love is in the way someone does not give up, even when the world says it would be easier to let go. It is in the way they choose to stand beside another, even when life tests their patience, their faith, their endurance. It is in the way someone holds another through their pain, through their heartbreak, through the moments that make them question everything. It is in the way they become a safe place, a shelter from the chaos, a reminder that no matter how hard things get, they will never have to face it alone. Love is in the way someone fights for another, not just in words, but in actions, in presence, in the unwavering promise that they will not walk away when the road gets rough. It is in the way someone kneels in prayer for the one they love, lifting them up when they are too tired to do it for themselves. It is in the way they carry the weight of another's burdens, not because they have to, but because love makes them want to. Love is in the way someone chooses patience over frustration, forgiveness over resentment, faith over fear. It is in the way they stand firm when life tries to shake them, in the way they refuse to let go even when everything feels uncertain. It is in the way they whisper, "I still believe in you," when doubt creeps in. It is in the way they see the goodness in another even when they cannot see it in themselves. Love is not just about being present in the good times, but in the times of sorrow, in the moments of grief, in the spaces where hope seems too distant to grasp. It is in the way someone stays up through the night, comforting a soul weighed down by worry. It is in the way they make sacrifices, not out of obligation, but because love is selfless, love is strong, love endures. It is in the way someone continues to love, even when it is tested by distance, by hardship, by the things that try to pull them apart. It is in the way they show up, time and time again, proving that love is not just something spoken, but something lived. Love is in the way someone fights for a relationship when the world tells them to walk away. It is in the way they hold on to hope, even when everything says to give up. It is in the way they carry another's heart as if it is the most precious thing in the world, protecting it, cherishing it, never taking it for granted. Love is in the way someone supports another's dreams, even when they do not fully understand them. It is in the way they choose to see the best in another, even when life has made it difficult. It is in the way they love, not just when it is easy, but when it requires strength, patience, and unwavering faith. It is in the way someone chooses to stay, to fight, to believe, even when the world gives them every reason to do otherwise. Love is in the way someone holds another's hand in a hospital room, in the way they wipe away tears without asking for an explanation, in the way they sit in silence when words are not enough. It is in the way someone takes another's pain and makes it their own, standing in the gap, refusing to let them face their struggles alone. It is in the way they whisper, "I will never leave you," and prove it over and over again. It is in the way someone learns to love through the seasons of hardship, understanding that real love is not about perfection, but about perseverance. It is in the way they stand beside another through financial struggles, through losses, through disappointments, never making them feel alone in the battle. It is in the way someone makes love a refuge, a safe place where the weary can find rest. It is in the way they remind another of their worth when life has made them feel small. Love is in the way someone says, "I am with you," and means it—not just in the good moments, but in the ones that test their commitment, their endurance, their heart. It is in the way they whisper, "I choose you," every single day, even when life makes it difficult. It is in the way they stand in the storm with another, refusing to leave when the winds are strong, when the waters rise, when the trials feel endless. It is in the way they anchor another in faith when doubts threaten to take hold. It is in the way they never let love be something fragile, but something that withstands the pressure, something that does not break under the weight of hardship. Love is not found in the absence of trials, but in the way it remains in the middle of them, unwavering, unshaken, immovable. It is in the way someone whispers, "I will love you through this," and holds on tighter when life tries to loosen their grip. It is in the way someone finds beauty in the struggles, seeing love not as something that fades in the hard moments, but something that shines even brighter because of them. It is in the way love becomes a source of strength, a reason to keep going, a reminder that even in the darkest nights, someone is standing beside them, lighting the way forward. It is in the way love does not run, does not falter, does not turn away when things are not easy. It is in the way love chooses faithfulness when others would walk away. It is in the way someone learns to love even when tested, even when stretched, even when exhausted. Love is in the way someone carries another's pain as if it were their own, in the way they find ways to make the burdens lighter, in the way they bring laughter into moments of sorrow. It is in the way they create a place where someone feels safe enough to be vulnerable, to be honest, to let down their walls. Love is in the way someone whispers, "I see you. I hear you. I will not leave." It is in the way someone forgives, over and over again, because love is not about holding onto mistakes, but about choosing grace. It is in the way someone refuses to let another feel abandoned, in the way they choose love even when life makes it difficult. Love is in the way someone stands at the finish line, cheering for another's victory as if it were their own. It is in the way they celebrate the triumphs, knowing they have walked through the battles together. It is in the way someone's presence alone can bring comfort, can bring peace, can bring healing to a weary heart. It is in the way someone never stops choosing another, through the laughter, through the tears, through the unexpected trials that life brings. It is in the way they find strength in one another, in the way they lift each other up, in the way they build something unbreakable. Love is not just in the moments of ease, but in the moments of endurance, in the times when choosing love is a decision, a commitment, a promise that does not waver. It is in the way love whispers, "I will stand beside you through it all," and proves it, time and time again. And perhaps, in the end, love is not just in the triumphs, but in the trials, in the way it stands firm, in the way it weathers every storm, in the way it becomes a song of strength, a stanza that carries us through even the hardest of days.

Chapter 10 - Between the Lines of Forever

Discovering love in the details of life.

Love is not just in the big moments, the milestones, the grand declarations that the world notices and celebrates. It is in the quiet, everyday details, the small things that seem insignificant but are woven together to create something beautiful and lasting. Love is in the way someone remembers how another takes their coffee, in the way they know which songs make them smile, in the way they instinctively reach for their hand when crossing the street, as if their touch alone is enough to say, "I've got you." Love is in the gentle way one person leans their head against another's shoulder after a long day, in the way they adjust the pillow just right before the other falls asleep, in the way they pull a blanket over them when they don't even realize they are cold. It is in the way someone whispers "Drive safe" before they leave, in the way they text, "Did you eat today?" because they know the other forgets when they are busy, in the way they notice the weariness in their voice even when they are pretending to be okay. Love is in the way one person always makes sure to save the last bite of something good, not because they don't want it, but because they know the other does. It is in the way they notice when their hands are cold and instinctively reach to warm them, in the way they gently tuck a stray piece of hair behind their ear, in the way they let their fingers linger just a second longer when they hold them, as if memorizing the feeling of their presence. Love is not just in the extraordinary, but in the ordinary moments that make up a life—waking up beside the same person every morning and choosing them again and again, noticing the way their voice changes when they are excited, recognizing the small shifts in their mood before they even say a word. It is in the way someone makes space for another, not just physically, but in their heart, in their life, in their dreams. It is in the way they instinctively reach for them in the middle of the night, in the way their breath slows when they are near, in the way their heartbeat settles simply because they are with the one who feels like home. Love is in the way someone lingers just a moment longer before saying goodbye, in the way they turn back for one last look, in the way they whisper "I miss you" even before the person has walked away. It is in the way someone notices the small things—the way their laughter sounds just a little different when they are truly happy, the way they tuck their hands into their sleeves when they are cold, the way they look at the sky as if it holds all the answers. It is in the way someone listens, not just to words, but to what is left unsaid, in the way they notice the sadness in another's silence, in the way they instinctively pull them closer when they need it most. Love is in the details, in the way someone's name sounds softer when spoken by the one who loves them, in the way their eyes light up when they hear a familiar voice, in the way their body naturally leans toward the person who feels safest. It is in the way someone keeps little notes, old photographs, small trinkets that hold memories others might forget, but they cherish because love is not just about moving forward, but about holding on to the moments that shaped them. It is in the way someone places a protective hand on another's back in a crowded place, in the way they make sure they always have their favorite snack, in the way they sit a little closer when they know the other needs to feel less alone. Love is in the pauses, in the spaces between words, in the deep breaths before saying something difficult. It is in the way someone remembers what makes the other nervous and reassures them before they even ask, in the way they say, "I'm proud of you," on the days they know the other needs to hear it most, in the way they believe in them even when they struggle to believe in themselves. Love is not just about being there for the big things, but about showing up for the little things, day after day, proving in quiet ways that the heart can speak louder than words ever could. It is in the way someone watches over another as they sleep, in the way they reach for their hand under the table, in the way they laugh at their jokes, even when they've heard them a hundred times before. It is in the way someone recognizes the way their voice softens when they are tired, in the way they make sure their shoes are by the door so they don't trip in the morning, in the way they instinctively shift to make room for them in every part of their life. Love is in the way someone lets another rest their head on their chest and runs their fingers through their hair absentmindedly, in the way they let them steal the blankets, in the way they always notice when something is wrong, even when the other insists that everything is fine. It is in the way someone slows down their pace to match the person walking beside them, in the way they always take the time to say goodnight, in the way they hold onto them just a second longer, as if trying to press the feeling of forever into the moment. Love is in the way someone notices the nervous habits the other has—the way they fidget when they are anxious, the way they bite their lip when they are deep in thought, the way they blink faster when they are trying not to cry. It is in the way someone leans in just a little closer when the world feels overwhelming, in the way they press their forehead against theirs as if grounding them, in the way they whisper, "I'm here," and mean it. Love is in the details, in the small, ordinary moments that may not seem like much, but are everything. It is in the way someone leaves their favorite mug on the counter because they know it's the first one they reach for in the morning, in the way they adjust the seat in the car before they drive because they know exactly how the other likes it, in the way they notice when their favorite song comes on and turn the volume up without saying a word. It is in the way someone gently rubs their back when they are having a hard day, in the way they whisper "You're not alone," in the way they find little ways to remind them that they are loved. Love is in the way someone keeps their promises, not just in the big ways, but in the small ways—showing up when they said they would, remembering the things that matter, proving over and over again that love is something that lives in the details. It is in the way someone notices when the other is struggling and takes their hand without hesitation, in the way they whisper, "You don't have to carry this alone," in the way they never let them feel like a burden. Love is in the way someone leaves the light on just a little longer when they know the other is afraid of the dark, in the way they keep a picture of them in their wallet, in the way they trace the lines of their palm absentmindedly, as if memorizing every part of them. Love is in the way someone holds another's face in their hands and looks at them like they are the most precious thing in the world, in the way they make them feel safe enough to be vulnerable, in the way they love every version of them, not just the easy ones. Love is not just about forever in the big sense of the word—it is about the moments in between, the everyday ways love is shown, the little details that make up a life shared together. It is about noticing, about cherishing, about finding beauty in the ordinary. Because in the end, love is not just about the grand gestures or the milestones, but about the moments that fill the spaces between—the ones that may not always be written down, but are always felt, always remembered, always treasured. Love is in the details, in the quiet moments, in the spaces between the lines, and that is where forever truly lives.

Chapter 11 - The Sonnet of Us

A timeless composition of hearts entwined.

Love is a song that never fades, a melody woven into the fabric of time, a sonnet that echoes in the hearts of those who choose to walk through life hand in hand, bound by something deeper than words, stronger than fleeting emotion. It is not just found in the grand moments that the world applauds, nor is it defined by the fireworks of passion that ignite and burn out too quickly. True love is a composition that lasts, a timeless piece written in the quiet rhythms of everyday life, where two souls find their harmony in the simple, beautiful act of choosing each other over and over again. It is in the way one person memorizes the other's favorite things—not because they have to, but because love makes them want to. It is in the way they instinctively reach for their hand in a crowd, in the way they press a gentle kiss to their forehead when no one is watching, in the way they whisper "You are my favorite place to be." Love is found in the way one person finishes the other's sentences, in the way they hear the hesitation in their voice and know exactly what they are trying to say without them needing to find the words. It is in the way they pull them close in the middle of the night, in the way they linger in an embrace as if holding onto time itself, in the way their presence alone is enough to turn an ordinary moment into something unforgettable. Love is written in the way someone slows their steps to match the other's pace, in the way they place a protective hand on their back, in the way they remember the little things—the stories they tell over and over, the way their eyes sparkle when they are excited, the way their hands tremble when they are nervous. It is in the way one person waits for the other, patiently, faithfully, knowing that love is not about rushing but about walking together, side by side, through every chapter, through every high and low. It is in the way someone whispers "I believe in you" when self-doubt creeps in, in the way they see beauty in their flaws, in the way they remind them, again and again, that they are loved just as they are. Love is not just in the words spoken but in the pauses between them, in the glances exchanged across a room, in the way two people can sit in silence and still hear everything they need to know. It is in the way someone makes space for another, not just in their home, but in their heart, in their dreams, in their forever. It is in the way they say "Take your time" when the world feels overwhelming, in the way they reach across the table just to touch their hand, in the way they whisper "I will always choose you." Love is in the way someone never lets the other feel alone, in the way they stand by their side, even when the weight of life feels heavy, in the way they become a refuge, a safe place, a home in a world that is constantly changing. It is in the way someone remembers the way they take their coffee, the way they hum their favorite song under their breath, the way they tuck a blanket around them when they are too tired to notice. Love is in the way one person recognizes another's silent battles, in the way they offer comfort without needing to be asked, in the way they show up, time and time again, proving that love is not just about staying when it is easy, but about holding on when it is hard. It is in the way someone traces the lines of another's hand as if memorizing a masterpiece, in the way they listen—not just to words, but to the things left unspoken, to the dreams whispered in the dark, to the fears that have never been voiced aloud. Love is in the way someone's voice softens when they say their name, in the way they find beauty in their laugh, in the way they never tire of hearing their stories, even the ones they have heard a hundred times before. It is in the way they tuck notes into their pocket just to make them smile, in the way they make ordinary days feel like poetry, in the way they hold onto every moment as if it is the most precious thing in the world. Love is in the way one person fights for another, not with anger, but with patience, with kindness, with the unshakable belief that love is worth every effort. It is in the way they catch them when they stumble, in the way they hold them when they are breaking, in the way they whisper "You don't have to do this alone." Love is in the way someone stays up late just to listen, in the way they run their fingers through another's hair absentmindedly, in the way they wrap their arms around them from behind just to remind them that they are loved. It is in the way they remember every little detail—not because they are trying, but because love makes them notice, love makes them cherish, love makes them see another person fully, completely, with all their imperfections and still find them extraordinary. It is in the way someone looks at another as if they are the most beautiful thing they have ever seen, in the way their soul feels lighter in their presence, in the way they feel safe enough to be their truest self without fear. Love is in the way someone traces the freckles on another's skin like constellations, in the way they whisper "I'm so grateful for you" in the quiet moments, in the way they let their guard down because love has made them brave. It is in the way one person stands in the rain just to be close to the other, in the way they wait at the airport gate with arms wide open, in the way they turn back for one last glance before walking away, as if afraid to miss even a second of what they have together. It is in the way someone fights for forever, in the way they never stop choosing love, in the way they write their story not in fleeting emotions but in the daily acts of devotion, in the ordinary moments that become the most cherished of all. Love is not about finding perfection, but about embracing the imperfect and making it beautiful. It is about knowing that the best love stories are not written in grand gestures, but in the details—the way someone touches another's face as if they are memorizing it, the way they wait in the driveway just to watch them drive away safely, the way their heartbeat slows when they hold them close. Love is in the way someone leaves their heart open, even when it has been hurt before, in the way they keep choosing to believe in love, in the way they let themselves be known completely and still find themselves loved in return. It is in the way someone builds a life with another, not just in big ways, but in all the little ones—the shared cups of coffee, the inside jokes, the way they always find their way back to each other no matter what. It is in the way they know that love is not about waiting for the perfect moment, but about creating beauty in the messy, unpredictable, wonderful reality of life together. It is in the way they hold hands as if holding onto forever, in the way they dance in the kitchen just because, in the way their love becomes a melody that never stops playing. It is in the way someone writes love into every moment, in the way they make time stand still with a single glance, in the way their love becomes a timeless composition, a song that will never fade. Love is not just about saying "I love you," but about proving it, about showing up, about choosing to write the story together, page by page, verse by verse, knowing that what they are creating is something beautiful, something unbreakable, something that will last long after everything else has faded. Love is the sonnet of two hearts entwined, a song that will never be forgotten, a masterpiece that time cannot erase.

Chapter 12 - Love in Every Chapter

A story that never stops unfolding.

Love is not a single moment, not just a beginning or an ending, but an ongoing story that never stops unfolding, a journey written in the details of everyday life, in the whispered words and quiet gestures, in the way two hearts continue choosing each other through every season, through every page, through every unexpected twist. Love is a story filled with laughter and sorrow, triumphs and trials, dreams and disappointments, yet through it all, it remains a story worth telling, worth living, worth cherishing. It is in the way one person remembers the other's favorite song, in the way they tuck a blanket around them when they are too tired to notice, in the way they make space for each other in the small routines of life—not because they have to, but because love compels them to. Love is in the way someone reaches for another's hand in the middle of a crowded room, not out of necessity, but because their touch alone is a quiet reassurance that says, "I am here." It is in the way their voice softens when they speak each other's names, in the way they turn toward each other in sleep without realizing it, in the way their presence alone is enough to make an ordinary day feel special. Love is in the way someone saves the last bite of dessert without being asked, in the way they turn the volume down because they know the other is sleeping, in the way they instinctively lean closer when the world feels too loud. It is in the way someone stands by another's side, not just when things are easy, but when life is heavy, when everything feels uncertain, when the future is unclear but love remains steadfast, a constant presence in the middle of the unknown. Love is in the way someone remembers the things that matter—the way their laughter sounds when it is genuine, the way their eyes sparkle when they talk about something they love, the way they bite their lip when they are deep in thought. It is in the way they notice the little changes, the way they sense when the other is carrying something heavy, the way they know when to speak and when to simply hold them close. Love is in the way someone waits when the other needs time, in the way they give space without making it feel like distance, in the way they listen—not just to words, but to the emotions behind them, to the things that go unsaid, to the unspoken hopes and fears that linger between conversations. It is in the way they whisper "You're not alone" when the world feels overwhelming, in the way they fight for each other, not with raised voices, but with patience, with understanding, with the choice to love even when things are not perfect. Love is found in the way two people share the simple, unremarkable moments of life, in the way they fold laundry together, in the way they exchange sleepy smiles over morning coffee, in the way they sit in comfortable silence, completely at peace in each other's presence. It is in the way someone stands in the doorway just a little longer before leaving, in the way they turn back for one last glance, in the way they hesitate before hanging up the phone, as if reluctant to let the moment end. Love is in the way someone sees beyond the surface, in the way they recognize the beauty in another's imperfections, in the way they choose to love not just the easy parts, but every part, every flaw, every scar, every fear. It is in the way they say "I still choose you" every single day, not because they have to, but because love is something worth choosing, something worth holding onto, something worth fighting for. Love is in the way someone stands beside another through the changing seasons, through the chapters that are filled with uncertainty, through the moments that test their strength, their patience, their devotion. It is in the way they believe in each other, in the way they encourage, in the way they lift each other up when the weight of life feels too heavy to carry alone. It is in the way they laugh together, in the way they cry together, in the way they hold on, knowing that their love is not just a fleeting moment, but a story that continues, page after page, chapter after chapter. It is in the way someone whispers "I'm here" in the quiet moments, in the way they press a kiss to their forehead as if sealing a promise, in the way they wrap their arms around them and make the world feel safe. Love is not just in the big gestures, in the grand declarations, in the perfect moments captured in photographs; it is in the everyday, in the little things that might seem insignificant to anyone else, but mean everything to the one who is paying attention. It is in the way someone instinctively knows when the other needs comfort, in the way they reach for them in the middle of the night, in the way they remember which side of the bed they prefer, in the way they adjust the thermostat because they know the other always gets cold first. It is in the way someone saves the movie they have been waiting to watch because they want to experience it together, in the way they send a text just to say "I love you" in the middle of the day, in the way they make time for each other even when life is busy. It is in the way someone fights for forever, not in words, but in actions, in the consistent, unwavering presence that says "I am not going anywhere." It is in the way they know each other's habits—the way they tap their fingers to a certain rhythm when they are thinking, the way they tilt their head when they are listening, the way they fidget when they are nervous. It is in the way someone notices the sadness in another's smile, in the way they hear the exhaustion in their voice, in the way they recognize when they need a moment to breathe. Love is in the way someone lifts another's chin when they are feeling defeated, in the way they stand beside them when the world feels unkind, in the way they remind them of their worth even when they cannot see it for themselves. It is in the way someone holds space for another, not just in the good times, but in the hard ones, in the moments when words fail, in the moments when love is not about what is spoken, but about what is felt. Love is in the way someone stays, in the way they fight for what matters, in the way they choose to walk through life together, knowing that their story is still unfolding, that every page is another opportunity to love more deeply, to give more freely, to cherish the moments that make up a lifetime. It is in the way someone forgives, in the way they see the best in each other, in the way they never stop believing that love is worth the effort, worth the patience, worth everything. It is in the way someone finds poetry in the mundane, in the way they make ordinary moments feel extraordinary, in the way they hold onto the love they have built together, knowing that it is not just a chapter, but the whole story. Love is not just about how it begins, or even how it ends—it is about everything in between, about the moments that may not seem significant at first but become the memories that matter the most. It is about the way love continues, in the way it grows, in the way it deepens, in the way it refuses to fade. It is about knowing that love is not just a moment, not just a feeling, but a choice, a journey, a story that never stops unfolding. And in the end, love is not just about the pages that have already been written, but about the ones still waiting to be lived.

Conclusion

Love is not a single moment, nor is it a fleeting feeling that comes and goes with time. Love is a masterpiece of quiet moments, of soft whispers, of hands reaching for each other in the dark. It is a story that does not end when the chapter closes but continues to be written in every sunrise shared, every promise kept, and every unspoken understanding between two hearts that have chosen to walk through life together. Love is the poetry of us—the verses written in the way we laugh, the stanzas formed in the way we hold each other a little longer, the rhythm found in the simple, sacred way we say "I am here."

As this book comes to an end, the love it speaks of does not. It lingers in the spaces between now and forever, in the memories of yesterday and the hopes of tomorrow. It reminds us that love is not just about the grand gestures, but about the little things—the warmth of a familiar voice, the way someone saves the last bite of dessert, the way an ordinary day becomes extraordinary simply because it is shared.

Love does not fade with time; it deepens, grows, and finds new ways to be expressed. It is found in the patience of understanding, in the grace of forgiveness, in the unwavering presence of someone who chooses you over and over again. Love is the kind of poetry that is not just written but lived, the kind of story that does not seek perfection but finds beauty in the imperfection of two hearts learning, growing, and loving together.

The poetry of us is not just in the past, nor is it something to be feared in the unknown future. It is here, now, in the breath between words, in the quiet moments that do not demand to be noticed but hold the weight of eternity within them. It is in the hands that hold on, in the eyes that say "I see you," in the hearts that refuse to let go.

And so, as we reach the final pages of this book, let it not be an ending, but an invitation—to notice love in the smallest of ways, to cherish the poetry that exists in every heartbeat, in every sigh, in every simple yet profound act of devotion. Because love, in its purest form, is a story that never truly ends.

This is the poetry of us. And it will always be written, always be spoken, always be felt—one quiet, beautiful moment at a time.

Don't miss out!

Visit the website below and you can sign up to receive emails whenever Joshua Rhoades publishes a new book. There's no charge and no obligation.

https://books2read.com/r/B-A-AJLBB-MTFYF

BOOKS 2 READ

Connecting independent readers to independent writers.

Did you love *The Poetry Of Us*? Then you should read *The Shepherd's Voice*[1] by Joshua Rhoades!

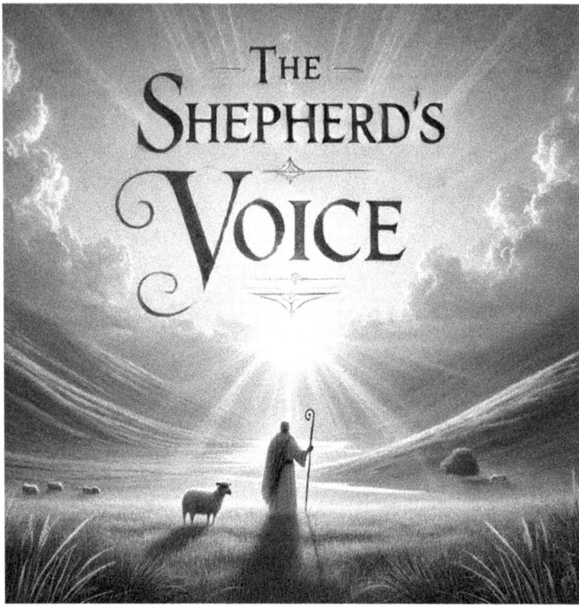

[2]

"The Shepherd's Voice" is a book designed to bring comfort, strength, and guidance to those seeking a closer walk with God. At its heart, this book celebrates the voice of the Shepherd—gentle, strong, and unwavering—that calls to each of us throughout our lives. Whether you're facing life's biggest challenges, or simply searching for peace in the day-to-day, "The Shepherd's Voice" offers insights and reflections to remind you that you are never alone. Through a blend of biblical wisdom, personal reflection, and inspiration, this book brings to life the

1. https://books2read.com/u/bpAvZk

2. https://books2read.com/u/bpAvZk

ways in which God's voice reaches out to us, guiding us like a shepherd leads his flock to green pastures and still waters.

Each chapter in "The Shepherd's Voice" explores a unique quality of the Shepherd's call, whether it's His comforting presence in times of trouble, His reassuring words in moments of fear, or His joyful guidance when we are lost. The book invites you to listen closely and find comfort in the knowledge that, no matter the season, the Shepherd's voice is ever-present, leading you toward peace, purpose, and a deeper faith. Each page is crafted to make readers feel encouraged and uplifted, providing gentle reminders of God's constant love and unshakable faithfulness.

This isn't just a book for difficult times, though it offers great solace to those who are struggling. "The Shepherd's Voice" is also a guide for joyful living, helping readers to embrace each day with renewed strength, hope, and faith. It is a testament to the power of listening to God's voice, to quieting the noise of the world, and allowing His words to refresh and restore our souls. You'll find encouragement to grow closer to the Shepherd, to understand His voice, and to lean on His wisdom as you walk your own unique path.

Through reflections on Scripture, moments of meditation, and timeless lessons on trust, faith, and courage, "The Shepherd's Voice" offers more than just words on a page—it offers a way to experience God's presence in a deeply personal and transformative way. Each chapter is an invitation to step away from worry, to lay down fears, and to find a lasting sense of peace and purpose. Just as a shepherd knows each sheep by name, the Shepherd knows us, and this book will help you experience that personal care and connection in a way that brings lasting hope.

"The Shepherd's Voice" is ideal for those looking to deepen their faith, for anyone feeling adrift and needing spiritual reassurance, or for readers simply wanting to reconnect with God's love and promises. It reminds us that we are valued and cared for by a loving Shepherd whose voice is always calling us toward a life of peace, grace, and fulfillment. So, if you're ready to be encouraged, inspired, and transformed, this book is your invitation to tune into the voice that has been with you all along—the voice of the Shepherd.

www.ingramcontent.com/pod-product-compliance
Ingram Content Group UK Ltd.
Pitfield, Milton Keynes, MK11 3LW, UK
UKHW041045101225
9485UKWH00039BA/292

9 798230 520115